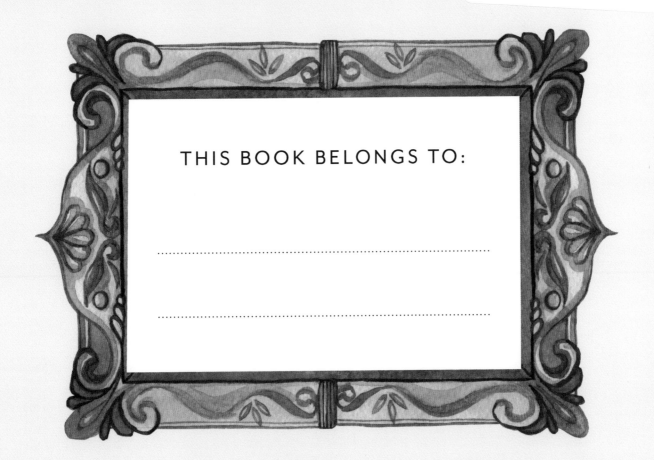

THIS BOOK BELONGS TO:

To my friends Val and June, thanks for the love, laughter and support over the years, and above all, for the memories. X

The Sparkly Crown
By Marie Darwin
Illustrated by Jan Syme

First published in 2021
Copyright Marie Darwin © 2021
All rights reserved.

ISBN: 978-1-8383245-0-6

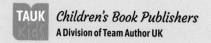

The Sparkly Crown

THE STORY OF HM QUEEN ELIZABETH II

BY MARIE DARWIN ILLUSTRATIONS BY JAN SYME

In 1926 in a house in London town, a baby was born who would become a princess, a queen and for the longest time be the monarch who would wear the sparkly crown.
Elizabeth and George were her proud parents and they said, "Our beautiful baby will be named Elizabeth, princess but not a queen and we will be happy in London town, and let Uncle David be the next to wear the sparkly crown."

Now Elizabeth was happy with mummy, daddy and a nanny to take care of her and she loved her dogs and horses and walking in the fresh air. When Elizabeth was 4 years old she got a lovely surprise, a baby sister called Margaret Rose with beautiful blue eyes.

The sisters loved to sing and
dance and never wear a frown.
"We will play together always,"
said Princess Margaret Rose,
"and let Uncle David be the next
to wear the sparkly crown."

When Princess Elizabeth was 10 years old, her poor old Grandpa England died and now Uncle David was going to be king. But then he fell in love, moved away and that changed everything.

And now Elizabeth's papa was going to be king, live in a palace in London town and wear the sparkly crown.

"Elizabeth, will you become Queen one day?" asked Princess Margaret Rose. "I suppose I will," said Elizabeth, "but one never really knows."

In 1939, the world was changing fast and there started a war all over the world. Elizabeth's home of London town was caught in all the blasts. The king and queen stayed in London and went to see these terrible sights and Elizabeth said, "Mummy, daddy, I promise when I am Queen, I will help the people with all my might; I will be proud to be from London town and make people proud of me, when I wear the sparkly crown."

The war went on till 1945 and Elizabeth helped by learning to drive. On the day the war ended, everyone wanted to celebrate and Princess Elizabeth crept out of the palace gate...

...into the crowd she went, joining in the fun and nobody recognised her, not one person, not one.

She said, "One day I will wear the sparkly crown, but just for today, I am going to celebrate in London town."

Just a year later Princess Elizabeth met a young man called Prince Philip of Greece and they started to fall in love, whenever they would meet.

Princess Elizabeth and Prince Philip were married in Westminster Abbey in 1947 and Elizabeth said, "One day I will wear the sparkly crown, but for today we are married, you are my husband and we will be happy and live in London town."

In 1948 Princess Elizabeth had a baby boy called Charles Philip Arthur George. Now Princess Elizabeth was very happy and so she had one baby more.

Princess Anne was a sister for Prince Charles and they shared their nursery toys in the house in London town. While Princess Anne wanted to be a great horsewoman when she grew up, Prince Charles knew he had to learn to be King and one day wear the sparkly crown.

In 1952, Princess Elizabeth's papa became ill and it was time for him to pass on the sparkly crown. Princess Elizabeth became Queen and lived in the big palace in London town. Queen Elizabeth said, "Papa, I will never let you down, now it is my turn to wear the sparkly crown."

The Queen's Coronation was the next year in 1953, and lots of people bought a television so they could watch and see.

"We are proud of our Queen," they said, "and we know that Elizabeth and Philip will never let us down." And all the children said, "Ooh, we wish we could wear the sparkly crown."

The 1960s saw a lot of changes for the Queen. First there were The Beatles and the Mersey Beat music scene. Then came the space rocket and the man on the moon, and when Armstrong stepped down the Queen said, "Wow, I never thought I would see this, when I first put on the sparkly crown."

The Queen also had some changes in her family life. She had two more baby boys in 1960 and 1964. The princes were called Andrew and Edward, and this took the Queen's children up to four.

The Queen said, "I love being a mother. I love my family life with my husband, children, horses and corgis at my feet. I do now feel that my family is complete. Now I can carry on as Queen, with all my family around, and I hope for a long time, I will continue to wear the sparkly crown."

In 1977, the Queen had a special anniversary and it was called the Silver Jubilee. It brought lots of street parties with jelly, ice cream and cups of tea. People celebrated all over the world though, not just in London town, because this meant that for 25 years, the Queen had worn the sparkly crown.

In the 1980s and 1990s there were a lot of
changes for the Queen with the sparkly crown.

Lots of happiness, sadness, weddings
and grandchildren passed through the
big palace in London town.

Then in 1999 there was a great party to celebrate the new millennium year, and Queen Elizabeth celebrated with all her family, and those she held quite dear. The people said, "Let's end the century with a cheer not a frown, and hip hip hurray for Queen Elizabeth, who always wears a smile as well as the sparkly crown."

ow from the year 2000 to 2015, Queen Elizabeth's family had grown and changed. Like a lot of families, happiness and sadness however the sun always comes out after the rain. This is what family means and things were no different for Elizabeth, just because she was the Queen.

Then in 2016, Queen Elizabeth became 90 years of age and sometimes still travelled the world from her home in London town. And now she has become the longest serving king or queen to wear the sparkly crown.

This is the story of Queen Elizabeth who wears the sparkly crown,
and lives in a palace in London town.

About the Author

Marie Darwin is a children's nursery nurse based in Liverpool. Marie is also a Liverpool tour guide and sometimes combines the two, giving young children a sense of culture and history about where they live and the wider world.

Marie is passionate about history and learning and after briefly meeting HM Queen Elizabeth II with her nursery children in 2016, she decided to use her talent of turning rhymes into stories by writing the story of the queen from birth to age 90.

At the time of publishing in 2021, Queen Elizabeth has been the reigning monarch for 69 years.

Marie has written two previous children's books:

What did Granddad Paul do when he was little? (Based on Paul McCartney - 2015)

John Lennon, the early years. (2017)

About the Illustrator

Jan Syme took up painting since retiring from work due to a life-changing injury.

Jan believes in focusing on what you can do and not what you can't do.

After discovering her talent as a pet artist, this is Jan's first venture into book illustration.

Jan first met the author when they both became involved in amateur dramatics.